E.A. Horton

Commemorating the Semi-Centenial Anniversary

Of the Dedication of the 1st Congregational Meeting-House, in Leominster

E.A. Horton

Commemorating the Semi-Centenial Anniversary
Of the Dedication of the 1st Congregational Meeting-House, in Leominster

ISBN/EAN: 9783337092412

Printed in Europe, USA, Canada, Australia, Japan

Cover: Foto ©ninafisch / pixelio.de

More available books at **www.hansebooks.com**

AN HISTORICAL ADDRESS.

COMMEMORATING

THE

SEMI-CENTENNIAL ANNIVERSARY,

OF THE

DEDICATION OF THE

1st Congregational Meeting-House,

IN LEOMINSTER.

DELIVERED WEDNESDAY, OCTOBER 15th, 1873,

BY

E. A. HORTON

Pastor of the First Congregational (Unitarian) Society.

PUBLISHED BY VOTE OF THE PARISH.

"ENTERPRISE OFFICE," LEOMINSTER, MASS.
1874.

To the Reader.

————◆◦◦◆►————

Appended to the main address are notes which provide the details of some transactions necessarily treated with brevity in the historical sketch. They are referred to by numbers in the text. Some portions omitted in the delivery of the address are now inserted. The work of preparing this brief record of a part of our religious past has been a labor of love. I offer it to my parishioners as an affectionate though slight expression ·of my interest in all things which pertain to them as individuals, or as a society. It was written at their request, and now appears in this form by their wish.

E. A. H.

ADDRESS.[1]

We are met to commemorate an event of no slight importance,

By nature man loves ancestral spots and historic scenes; he loves them though remote personages and indistinct deeds have contributed to their fame. How much warmer is his regard, then, for that which has been identified with his fathers, now asleep, and bound up with their declining and his opening course.

Time dims much to the heart, and quenches the light of many memories, but I have yet to find that person who lost, in advancing years, his esteem for the old sanctuary wherein worship first educated him; or who never desired again, when youth was past, to visit the sanctuary of his fathers. No! peculiar and tenacious is that tie. Those whose eyes have in manhood's prime beheld massive cathedrals, whose feet have later trod the aisles of gorgeous mosques, maintained unweakened firm allegiance to the homely aisles, the unpretending walls, of some modest church, nestled in a New England valley. For its associations and import no dazzling tabernacle could compensate. Time's hand has rolled the years in swift succession, since this meeting-house first echoed with praise and prayer. A little more than half a century ago the timbers of this building rose, sprung to their places by stalwart men. Fifty years ago, this day, a happy multitude gathered within these walls to dedicate them to the worship of a God of Love. The scene how changed! Scarcely any feature of the locality remains the same. Nothing indeed but the self-same sky, starry and sheltering. The ground abides, and nature's general aspects. The same strong beams exist, a semblance to the original framework survives in the structure. Yes! the same bell that rang fifty years ago, calling the town's people together, has summoned our glad steps. Not much more numerous are the links abiding among the present audience and that collected here in 1823. The men who toiled to make this goodly house have gone. Read their names on tablets in yonder resting-place. Here and there among you are those who were young men and young women, boys and girls, at that time. The actors in that scene half a century ago have vanished. Why do I re-call time's innovations? Surely not for sadness. To bet-ter esteem the dead. In honoring them we do invest ourselves with honor. They have their reward. We can-not do better than remember that they labored well when living, and we, to be worthy of their spirit and deeds, must ourselves be emulous and noble. That is the main lesson of this evening hour. I am to speak to you this evening, as briefly as may be consistent with the subject, of our meeting-house. Not of the church as a body of communicants, not of the parish proper, not of doctrine, not of the birth and infancy of the society; our exercises centre around the existence of this sanctuary as a place of divine worship.

Yet it may be well to quickly trace up the historic line, of which this is the continuation, preceding the erection of this edifice. In doing this entire work, at your committee's request, I ask you to walk with me as one goes over a dusty road, relieved now and then by green spots of shade and beauty. We are to deal with statistics and unvarnished truth.

The earliest records of this town, that we possess, begin in 1740; on the first pages is the account of a meeting held by the scanty inhabitants, when the subject of a "meeting-house" was agitated.[2]   On Dec. 15, 1740, it was voted to build said meeting-house 50 feet in length, 40 feet in width, 23 feet in hight. These dimensions were afterwards curtailed by a succeeding vote at another meeting, and economy cut five feet from the length, five feet from the breadth, one foot from the hight.

This building was located on the north-west corner of what is now the old burying-ground.   A rough, un-painted, windowless structure, with no pews in it for many years.   Town meetings were held there.   This house the inhabitants of Leominster used for worship until 1775, when it became the property of a Baptist society in Harvard, who took it to pieces and reconstructed it in Still River. There it sheltered a congregation for a long time. In 1850 it was transformed into a parsonage, and remains yet a useful member of society. In 1773, when the storm of the revolution was thundering in the distance, Leominster voted to build a larger meeting-house. An acre and a little more of land was bought for the purpose, situated where now the common is, of Rufus Houghton. The dimensions of this structure were sixty feet in length by fifty in breadth. Its portals looked toward the rising sun. Eighteen square pews,—deep, broad, generous pews,—filled the body of the church, and thirty more ranged around the walls. Such was the edifice existing in 1816. It was situated on the spot where the flag-staff of the common stands. No fence ran around the spot. Scarcely any houses existed in the neighborhood. A modest building, it was designated when completed as an elegant meeting-house.

Usages peculiar to the ancient time prevailed in its service, — the lining of hymns, the rising at prayers, and clapping of the seats, — the deacons in their wigs sat beneath the pulpit on a bench named from them,— children rolled on the floor, hid from sight by the towering pews, — aged people stole naps in sermon time, encouraged by the protecting seats, — no fire broke the wintry chill, — the black man had his place assigned in a gallery corner, — the minister preached in a costume consisting of a large wig and high-topped boots, and above his head was a large sounding-board. Here and there watchful guardians of order moved about the congregation checking mirth, and subduing noise. No bell pealed the Sunday call; no clock told the swift hours. Let us see whose voices had spoken from the pulpit up to that time.

The Rev. John Rogers, the first minister of this society, was then dead. His embittered career ended. A character of no little originality, — with "an inquisitive spirit," said Dr. Bancroft of him,—honest and blunt, he is pictured to us as a man who suffered as those suffer who are placed by circumstances in a crisis, and map out new courses. He was cast out. He was ordained and installed Sept. 14th, 1743, (O. S.)[3] Mr. Rogers died Oct. 6, 1789, aged 78 years.

Succeeding Mr. Rogers came Rev. Francis Gardner, who enjoyed a long, calm pastorate of useful labor. He was a scholar, sought most the enforcement of plain, Christian truth, and gave but little attention to innovating ideas. His ordination and installation occurred Dec. 22, 1762.[4] Mr. Gardner died suddenly June 2, 1814, aged 79 years. He was lamented by all; at his funeral, as an eye witness informs me, the procession extended from the parsonage, standing where now the Salisbury house is, to the church, six deep, every one walking in close ranks.

We are thus brought down to the Rev. William Bascom, whose settlement took place May 10th, 1815.[5]

c

It was during Mr. Bascom's stormy pastorate, in May 1816, when a committee appointed for the purpose, reported to the town on the advisability of altering and enlarging the old meeting-house. Mr. Bascom was a man of progress, a liberal mind. He did not please all. His sermons were characterized as weak, his prayers able. He withdrew from his position in 1820, and died in 1845.

I have thus brought you down to the time embracing the preliminaries attending the building of this sanctuary. I will quote the words of the committee, to whom was referred the subject of a new house of worship. "Comparing" they say, "the great and increasing number of the inhabitants with the comparitive small size of the Meeting-House, and that although a large proportion of the people are well accommodated with seats, yet your committee view with regret that from want of sufficient room, there are a considerable number who are obliged to pay a price for their accommodations far beyond what either reason or former example would justify, whilst another part of the inhabitants cannot be accommodated with seats at any price, and considering that those two last classes of citizens, — the first from becoming weary of paying an exorbitant price for their seats, and the other from being unable to procure any, — may be induced to abandon the place of public worship in this town and to seek one elsewhere, where they may be accommodated on reasonable terms. For these and other considerations, your committee are unanimous in opinion that the Meeting-House, in its present state, is insufficient for the town. Your committee find on examination that the frame of the Meeting-House is in every part sound and good, and is capable of being enlarged in such a manner as to be a handsome and convenient house. They therefore recommend that the present Meeting-House be enlarged to sixty feet by seventy, with a belfry in front, which your committee believe will afford ample accommodations for the inhabitants." They then add, "It is our opinion that if the town see fit to enlarge the present Meeting-House, it would be better to remove it from its present situation, as an enlargement where it now stands would occupy too much of the common ground, now too small."

Two locations presented themselves favorably, so the report continues, which I must abridge. One being that owned by Capt. Hale, about an acre of land filled at this day by Mr. J. C. Allen's residence and store. It was purchasable for $200. The other was land owned by the heirs of Metaphor Chase, being that territory now occupied by this house, the Town Hall, Baptist Church, and some adjacent ground, then tenanted only by a house once used as an inn, and some stables. Its area was two acres and fifty rods; this was available at the price of $2000. The committee warmly urged the purchase of the second lot of land. Subdivisions for sale, eligibility of location, disposal of buildings then on it for good prices, sheltered site in winter, — these inducements they presented strongly and wound up with this glowing sentence, that "such a choice would add greatly to the beauty, elegance, and respectability of the town." Signed by Abraham Haskell, Chairman. This report was recommitted with instructions to consider the expediency of building a new Meeting-House entirely, and six individuals were added to the committee.

In August 1816, this land was purchased of the heirs of Metaphor Chase, at the price of $2000. At the meeting of May 5th, 1817, another report was submitted as follows : "It is unanimously deemed expedient by the committee that the town should build a new Meeting-House, to be completed for public worship in three years from that time." This was accepted by 66 votes for, and 32 against it.

Whether brick or wood should be employed as material in the construction of the house was considered; wood was chosen for its cheapness. The building committee was chosen Dec. 24, 1821, and general instructions given to them by the town. Their names are as follows : Solomon Strong, Jonas Kendall, Joel Crosby, Bezaleel Lawrence, William Burrage, Rufus Kendall, Israel Nichols, William Carter, Charles Hills. These were elected on one ballot. By a succeeding vote, Abel Carter and John Taylor were added. Additional committees were afterwards chosen for different purpose; they consisted of Joseph G. Kendall, William Perry, Levi Nichols, Abraham Haskell, Jr., John Buss, Jr., Jonathan Merriam and David Wilder. The final vote to build this Meeting-

House was fifty-nine to forty-one, and then by rallying voters the list stood 'eighty-three affirmative and forty-nine negative.

In January, 1822, the appointed committee reported their plan. The structure was to be 75 feet long, 62 feet wide, and, as they stated it, — the end to be in front — the pulpit at the opposite end; 10 feet of the front to be made into a porch; three doors from porch into interior. Colonnade 32 feet high, above it a belfry, above the belfry a spire; 88 pews were to fill the body of the house and 48 the galleries, making in all 136. The cost really exceeded the estimate by only four hundred dollars.

The discussion on the exact location of the building, how it should stand to the compass, was sharp. One vote was passed by fifty-eight to fifty-seven; this was reconsidered, and after much battling, that point, seemingly smaller than much else, was settled. It is always thus in human affairs, transient contests are the fiercest.

The Aurora Lodge of free and accepted masons, then located here, now at Fitchburg, was invited to lay the corner stone according to immemorial usage. The invitation was accepted, and preparations made for the event, the Lodge suggesting a particular day. [6] The suggestions of the Lodge did not prevail. No doubt many were opposed to the whole matter and their influence carried the point for selecting the 10th of June, as the day. Upon this the Masons by another vote in May asked.

for release from their promise and declared it impossible · to prepare properly for the occasion as soon as that day. Therefore we may conclude that the corner stone was laid on the 10th of June, according to the town's decision, but with what, if any ceremonies, I am not able to learn.

The day of raising the frame was a memorable one. It was in the pleasant month of June. Many are now living who vividly recall that occasion. Each timber was in readiness; selected men awaited orders, and a guarding rope kept back the crowd. Capt. Legate was there, his sea-faring skill having marked him as the one to direct the affair.

All went well. Ropes creaked beneath the unusual burden and the sound of the hammer resounded continually. Pails of grog were emptied by the heated workmen, for in those days liquor was all too freely used. Everything seemed prosperous until on the second day an impending disaster hung for a moment over the work. Staunch ropes, pulled by strong men, were elevating the belfry to its place. Slowly it rose to an upright position; hundreds of eyes were on it; gradually it reached the position destined for it when to the dismay of all it sank back and threatened to fall. A feeling of fear, a sinking at the heart filled all. But the voice of Capt. Legate was heard. "Bring it up men, bring it up to its place;" and that man who had used the trumpet on many a stormy deck, spake then, and the belfry rose again until it poised its base firmly on the colonnade. A cheer went up, loud and long, from the spectators. An eye witness informs me of one other threatened accident which was happily averted. John C. Kendall was on the edge of the belfry after it had been raised, pounding the beams into better places with his sledge hammer, when he struck his body against a man, Joel Dresser, passing behind, and losing his balance, was just falling over to the ground, to meet a sure death, when the person against whom he struck seized his clothing and held him. It was a narrow escape. Upon being urged to go down, young Kendall declared that he was not frightened and should stay as long as the rest stayed.

The contractor for this edifice was Mr. Cutting. The Meeting-Houses in Templeton and Northborough are also testimonies to his thorough workmanship. Enter the upper part of this building and you will find great timbers and sound timbers; this structure is strong in its half-century age. Mr. Cutting was an honest contractor, which is more than we can say of many in this day.

During 1823, before the building was completed, Joel Crosby, Esq., presented the town with a bell and Capt. Barker transported it free of charge from Boston, which in those days was no trivial kindness. This pleasant bell now strikes the hours for us daily, and calls us to our Sunday worship. An inscription was placed upon it acknowledging the giver, and he was asked by vote of the town to select whatever pew he wished in the new Meeting-House, at the appraisal, before any had been sold at auction. This Mr. Crosby did and took pew number 4.

Eight thousand dollars were assessed on the pews, to be raised by their sale. The day of their disposal came in September, 1823. Work was finished; it was now one year and a half since the inaugural digging was commenced. The auctioneer was instructed to receive no bids for a pew under twenty-five cents. No person should purchase more than one pew for himself. Brisk and successful was the sale. Sixteen hundred dollars above the fixed sum was realized. At the conclusion only one pew, number 16, remained unbought. So needful was the town of church accommodations that in October of the same year additional pews were made.

And now approached the day of dedication. The Rev. Abel Conant, then minister of the town, was requested to preach a sermon on Sunday afternoon, October 12th, on leaving the old Meeting-House, and one on Wednesday afternoon succeeding, October 15th, to dedicate the new Meeting-House.

Rev. Mr. Conant followed Mr. Bascom. He was a writer of excellent sermons, of good character, but not animated in the pulpit. I myself have read some of his discourses, feeling that for expression and graceful style, they compare well with modern ones. To him also the sports of the wood and field were agreeable. His hand was acquainted with the gun, and his pliant rod often landed the trout upon the brook's bank. His ordination and installation occurred January 24th, 1821.[7]

The dedication day was pleasant. A throng attended. It was of universal interest. Each sermon, the one on leaving the old, the one on entering the new Meeting-House, was afterwards printed. They survive in many homes. Appended to the dedication is a note of the services written by one present. The introductory prayer was made by Rev. Mr. Damon of Lunenburg, the dedicatory prayer by Rev. Dr. Thayer of Lancaster, the concluding prayer by Rev. Mr. Osgood of Sterling. Mr. Conant's sermon was from the text, "And the disciples were called Christians first in Antioch." Acts XI—26. His text for the farewell sermon in the old Meeting-House on the common, was this; "And when the cloud was taken up from the tabernacle, then after that the children of Israel journeyed." Numbers IX—17. We can imagine the bass viol sending forth its most sonorous tones, and the pitch pipe of the chorister giving the key. Perhaps the bass singer was there who had sung so long in the old church. Of him it was said, so good and devout a man was he, that whenever he reached a word in the hymn especially pious, he hung to it so long that he made discord. It was said, at least by a member present at the time, and recorded, that several pieces of sacred music were sung in a style which did credit to the choir of singers in Leominster. The wigs of the deacons were well powdered that day; alert were the men who watched for noisy boys, and the maidens had on their best and fairest attire.

E

It was a solemn time also. Out of the old sanctuary they had gone, rich in memories, dear by associations. The novelty of the new could not obliterate the attachments to the old. It had been their religious home for nearly fifty years; now they were to say farewell to its walls forever. Change was to seize it, and the place where it had stood should know its presence no longer.

Established and at rest from their labors, the society now entered upon the enjoyment of their unwonted privileges. In April of the next year, the committee made a final report, submitting all the summings-up and total results, and concluded in these words: "Your committee knowing that the erection of a new Meeting-House was a great undertaking, but considering what our fathers have done for us and the benefit it would be to the rising generation and society, they proceeded, and by the blessing of a kind Providence prospered in the work of the house of the Lord. The liberality of great numbers in contributing labor in wharfing up the foundations of the Meeting-House, the union that prevailed in disposing of the seats, the prospect of the flourishing state of the society, and the zeal to support public worship afford your committee full satisfaction for their time and labor. Therefore your committee do not charge for their services."

The old Meeting-House was appraised by disinterested parties at four hundred and sixty-six dollars, including foundations, which was cheap enough, we may judge. It was taken to pieces and the most of its material used in constructing a Town House. This afterward became Gardner Hall, and served for school wants until 1869, when it was burned to the ground. Nothing now remains of that structure.

How to warm this house seemed to perplex the worthy people. In 1823 and '4 committee after committee was chosen, and every one resigned. The members of one, however, consulted and reported that they could not decide on any method. There must have been a strong admiration at that time for religion under difficulties. A native of this town has related to me his experience as a boy, of carrying a large box of coals up the broad aisle every Sunday morning for his grandmother's feet. How he dreaded it, and felt ashamed.

I find that in 1828 the town voted to rent the cellar beneath the audience room, and curious to know how much of an income this transaction furnished the society, I discovered the following entry: "Received of Solon Carter, Esq., for rent of cellar one year, $1.62 1-2!" Eight years after the erection of the building, examination was made to ascertain the cost of necessary repairs. So carefully and judiciously had the occupants treated it, that the report called for only ten dollars to cover main expenses. But four years after that satisfactory statement it was deemed necessary to pass a town vote creating a committee to watch "idle and mischievous boys who were defacing and destroying the public buildings."

The years rolled by; the town grew. That part of

the Puritan's plan which looked to the identification of Church and State gave way in Leominster, having grown weak by degrees for twenty years. The act which set this parish apart from the town, and gave it functions wholly its own, occurred on the fourth of May 1835. Only one of the petitioners is now living who applied for the right of incorporation; that surviving one is Ward M. Cotton. [8]

In 1837 several important events transpired affecting the Meeting-House and its people. Rev. Abel Conant died on the 6th of December, 1836, 43 years old. To his labors succeeded Rufus P. Stebbins, then fresh from the Divinity School. His installation was observed Sept. 20th, 1837. [9] About the time of his settlement a clock was placed in the belfry of the Meeting-House, a handsome pulpit Bible was presented by Mr. James G. Carter, and a clock for the interior was set up in front of the gallery, a gift from Mr. Joseph Woodward. The belfry clock, upon whose dials we now daily look, was partly and mostly a gift by the will of the late Joel Crosby, Esq., whose generous present of a bell had preceded his death.

Changes upon the pulpit were made not far from this time; the circular staircases were supplanted by direct ones. An additional pew was thus created on each side of the stairs. Not without interest to us, who decorously observe the service of Sunday, is the record of a vote by the parish selecting Mr. Solon Carter,

Emory Burrage and Gen. A. S. Gibbs, a committee to preserve order during divine worship. It is noticeable that two of these gentlemen sat in the singers' seats. In 1842 their duties must have increased, for three more were added, but in 1857 it was not deemed necessary to have but three and they were appointed to watch the galleries. Blinds were deemed advisable for the windows, provided they could be put on without any cost to the parish.

Piece by piece the parish has surrendered the ground which once stretched out so generously around the Meeting-House. The first important disposal was that of the ground now known as the common; the site of the old Meeting-House. In November, 1841, the transfer of it was made for six hundred dollars, to the town, under these conditions: That it shall never be used for any other purpose; never have buildings placed upon it; the privilege was allowed of enclosing it with a slight fence, if deemed advisable. These legal stipulations, now on record, will settle, I hope, the future of this small piece of green, and preserve it always from being made smaller, or from perverted uses by any parties.

Many years before the sale of this common to the town an important point of law was decided by the Supreme Court, affecting parish property. This test case occurred in 1826, being the first parish of Medford vs. Pratt. (4th Pickering, page 222. Rights of parishes to succeed towns in parochial capacity.) Town meetings

F

in Leominster had been excited over this question: Did
the first parish own the land which the town held before
the first parish was created? New religious societies had
sprung up and they naturally contested the claim of the
first parish to this property. The town was also desir-
ous to prove its title to the land, since it was in need
of some for public buildings. The Supreme Court had
decided that when a parish succeeded to a town in its
parochial capacity, it took possession of all lands formerly
held in trust for the use of town meeting-house and the
worshipers in it. This was of great significance. It
settled the main question, but there were never wanting
persons who sought to question the decision and evade it.
When the disposal of the common, and ground for the
town house and engine house came up, a hot and stir-
ring debate arose over the adjustment of the sale. A
committee was chosen by the town, consisting of one from
each Trinitarian society, viz: James Parker, of the Evangelical society, Seth Coggswell, of the Methodist, and
Micah R. Ball, of the Baptist. They were to consult
with a committee from the first Congregational Society,
composed as follows: Solomon Strong, Charles W. Wilder,
William Perry. As a result of the consultation, a report was rendered to the town, written by Judge Strong,
recommending that the first Parish go back six years
before the death of Mr. Chase and pay the interest on
two thousand dollars for that time; also, pay other claims
made by the town, making in all one hundred and ninety

two dollars and thirty-eight cents. Some claims on the part of the first parish were allowed, and the result was a friendly compromise in which the bitterness of controversy was buried.

In the year 1844, Mr. Stebbins brought his ministry in this town to an end by accepting a call to the charge of the Meadville Divinity School. Soon succeeding him came Hiram Withington, whose ordination in this house took place December 25th, 1844.[10] Withington's memory survives among this people as the memory of something musical and gentle survives. His record was that of a brilliant, loving character, whose frail body broke before strong energies. He died October 30th, 1848, having retired from the pulpit some time previous.

A call extended to the Rev. Amos Smith was accepted by him, and his installation was held on Sunday, November 26th, 1848.[11] Soon after Mr. Smith's coming, measures were launched to effect a complete remodelling of the Meeting-House. Consequently, on April 28th, 1849, the parish decided to appropriate forty-five hundred dollars towards a remodelling of the edifice, and chose for a committee to superintend the work, the following persons: Augustus Morse, James H. Carter, Abel Bowers, J. C. Allen, Ward M. Cotton. Fifteen hundred dollars were afterwards added to the original sum voted, making the whole appropriation six thousand dollars. The work of modernizing the church of '23 was successful. Changes came upon it more radical than those so lately introduced. The main floor was raised, a large vestry created, the pulpit cut down, frescoing introduced, and the pews shorn of their large proportions. Dr. Stebbins was invited to preach a discourse appropriate to the last day of worship in the old audience room, which he did. During the time of renovation, this society, by the kindness of the Evangelical society, held 'services in their Meeting-House. At last, on Thursday, February 28th, 1850, the improved edifice was re-dedicated. Mr. Henry Allen had generously presented the church with a Communion table and two chairs. They are now in use. From the Ladies' Benevolent Association was received money for lamps and fixtures.

A few years after the re-dedication a new organ was purchased; so well made was it that even now the tones and compass of the pipes are not easily excelled. A piano was also purchased for the vestry. Not until 1856 were hand-rails and balustrades placed along the entrance steps. In that year Mr. Smith resigned his charge, and on Wednesday, September 2d, of the following year, Stephen Barker was ordained and installed his successor.[12]

No changes in the house of worship occurred during Mr. Barker's pastorate. Additional pieces of land the parish had sold until over the once vacant spots a Baptist Meeting-House had risen, and the present Town Hall had sprung up. Ever enlarging and populating, the centre of the town presented altered aspects from its appearance in 1823.

Rev. Mr. Barker severed his relations with the society in 1860, and on the succeeding year, Wednesday, June 1st, Rev. Eli Fay was settled in his place.[13]

I find no records which refer to external changes during Mr. Fay's active ministry. The Meeting-House remained the same. In the year 1864, this pastor resigned and was followed by Rev. J. B. Green, whose installation occurred Wednesday, August 3d, of that year.[14]

During Mr. Green's service an elegant chandelier was procured and presented to the society. It has now been displaced by the different methods of lighting the audience room.

I have now brought you, my hearers, down to 1867, when Mr. Green ceased his service here; down to 1868, when your present pastor came. His ordination occurred Thursday, October 1st, of that year.[15]

Concerning the changes which have occurred in this Meeting-House since that time, I must speak, in order to fulfil my task. In 1870 an important step was taken by building the present Chapel, which now serves so well the wants of the society.[16] This portion of our house was dedicated December 1st, 1870. Forming no slight addition to the exterior form of the Meeting-House it has proven by its interior arrangements a very great improvement on the usefulness of the parish. A piano was permanently placed in the parlor; your pastor's study was generously filled with furnishings, gifts of valuable articles were placed in the kitchen, and now

G

but recently given, a fine array of pictures decorate the parlor walls, the gift of a former resident of this town. For much of all this we are indebted to the ladies.

In the spring of this year it was deemed best to again apply the hand of alteration to the audience room. For three months we worshiped in the public hall. With skill the committee, viz, Isaac Cowdrey, C. H. Merriam, George F. Morse, J. G. Tenney, and George E. Tisdale, superintended the work. On the first Sunday in August, the 3d of the month, we re-entered with songs and praise, our old home freshened and beautified.[17] On that day the services were conducted by Rev. R. R. Shippen. These changes you behold, — they are before you. I need not detail their extent or character. Of the gifts which accompany these alterations I would mention the fine Bibles and handsome table, contributed by Stow F. Haws, and the carpet which was from the ladies.

With as much mellowing of hard facts as I could achieve I have led you over that part of your history as a society relating to the Meeting-House. I have referred to the service of those whose voices have spoken to this people in the sermon's exhortation or the prayer's entreaty.[18]

Here I pause. More than full is my allotted space. If to me there is a fullness at heart, and a quick sense of gratitude, as I recount the signal mercies of God to this people, how much richer must be the emotion pervading the more aged; dwellers for half a century in this holy place. House of our fathers, we love thee! Altar where the saintly and pure have prayed; where the erring and sorrowful have found peace, — let no oblivion dim our affection for thee!

When time shall have levelled thy roof, or the hand of change smitten thee, O rise, beloved house, into some new and fairer form, to perpetuate thy blessings unto future generations, and bequeath thy dear memory to the children's children!

NOTES.

(1) The exercises commemorating the half century age of this Meeting-House occurred Wednesday evening, Oct. 15th, 1873. A social hour was spent in the Chapel rooms, after which, at 7 1-4 o'clock the people gathered in the audience room of the Meeting-House. A large congregation was present. The decorations of autumn leaves and flowers were beautiful. After an anthem by the choir, selections from scripture were read by Rev. E. J. Gerry, of Boston. Prayer was then offered by Rev. Geo. S. Ball, of Upton. Following these devotional services came the historical address by the pastor, herewith printed. Solon Carter then assumed the chair and called on the following gentlemen to address the meeting: Rev. Augustus Woodbury, of Providence, R. I., Rev. E. J. Gerry, of Boston, Benjamin Johnson, of Woonsocket, R. I., Rev. Geo. S. Ball, of Upton, and Rev. Seth Chandler, of Shirley. All but the first and last speakers were natives of Leominster. Their remarks were appropriate reminiscences of early days spent in the town, with allusions to the ancestors and influences of the church. Communications were read from Rev. Rufus P. Stebbins, D. D., Rev. Eli Fay, and Rev. Amos Smith, former pastors of the society, and from Prof. E. J. Young, of Cambridge, expressing regrets at their inability to be present, and extending cordial greetings. The exercises closed with a benediction by the pastor. Messrs. Solon Carter, J. C. Allen and C. H. Merriam constituted the committee under whose charge this semi-centennial observance was conducted, and all its arrangements perfected.

(2) The original founders of this church, from whose compact and aim sprang the Meeting-House, were these: John Rogers, Ebenezer Polley, James Boutelle, Thomas Houghton, Benj. Whitcomb, Thomas Wilder, Joseph Wheelock, Nathaniel Carter, Jonathan White, Ephraim Stone, Daniel Johnson, Simon Butler, Oliver Carter, Thomas White, Phillips Sweetzer, Gardner Wilder.

(3) At the ordination of Rev. John Rogers, Rev. Thomas Parker, of Dracut, preached the sermon; Rev. Daniel Rogers, of Littleton, offered the ordaining prayer; Rev. John Prentice, of Lancaster, gave the charge, and Rev. W. Hall, of Westford, extended the Right Hand of Fellowship.

(4) The following clergymen participated in the ordination of Rev. Francis Gardner: Rev. Mr. Smith, of Marlborough, preached the sermon; the opening prayer was offered by Rev. Mr. Harrington, of Lancaster; Rev. Mr. Gardner, of Stow, gave the charge; Rev. Mr. Goss, of Bolton, made the ordaining prayer and Rev. Mr. Swift, of Acton, gave the Right Hand of Fellowship.

II

(5) The order of exercises at the installation of Rev. Wm. Bascom was as follows: Rev. James Murdock, of Princeton, preached the sermon; Rev. John Cushing, of Ashburnham, gave the charge, and Rev. T. B. Gannett, of Cambridgeport, offered the Right Hand of Fellowship. The ordaining prayer, Rev. Dr. Abiel Holmes, of Cambridgeport, offered; Rev. Nathaniel Thayer, of Lancaster, made the introductory prayer, and the concluding one, Rev. Charles Wellington, of Templeton, offered

(6) Evidently the Lodge felt highly complimented by the request, if we may judge from the tone of the resolutions passed at a Lodge meeting, March 11, 1822, which I copy from their records:

Voted, that the thanks of Aurora Lodge be presented to the inhabitants of Leominster for the honor they have conferred in requesting the Lodge to take measures to lay the corner-stone of the new Meeting-House, about to be built in this town, according to ancient usages in such cases.

Voted, that the Lodge, with pleasure, do themselves the honor of complying with the request of the town.

Voted, that the Lodge, with due submission, will wait for the town to appoint the time, but at the same time beg leave to suggest that provided it should not incommode the town or the undertaking, it would be more convenient for the Lodge to perform the exercises on the 24th of June next."

(7) At the ordination of Rev. Abel Conant, Rev. Humphrey Moore, of Milford, N. H., preached the sermon; Rev. Dr. Nathaniel Thayer, of Lancaster delivered the charge; Rev. Thomas Bede, of Wilton, N. H., proffered the Fellowship of the churches, while to Rev. Reuben Puffer, D. D., of Berlin, fell the address to the people.

(8) The First Congregational Parish and Society, of Leominster, was organized the 4th day of May, 1835. The petition for the right to hold the meeting was signed by Ward M. Cotton, Amos Haws, Thomas Hills, Thomas G. Merriam, Bartemas Tenney, William Wilder, Artemas Bowers, Silas Allen, William Burrage, David Wilder, John Taylor, Bazaleel Lawrence, Charles W. Wilder.

(9) Exercises at the ordination of Rev. Rufus P. Stebbins. Prof. Henry Ware, Jr., of Cambridge, preached the sermon; Rev. Isaac Allen offered the ordaining prayer; Rev. Nathaniel Thayer, D. D., gave the charge; Rev. Calvin Lincoln extended the Right Hand of Fellowship; Rev. A. B. Muzzey delivered the address. The opening prayer was made by Rev. Mr. Osgood, of Sterling, and Rev. Joseph Allen, of Northborough, made the concluding prayer.

(10) At the ordination of Rev. Hiram Withington, Rev. Nathaniel Hall, of Dorchester, gave the sermon; Rev. Geo. Putnam, of Roxbury, the charge; Rev. J. H. Allen, of Jamaica Plain, the Hand of Fellowship. Rev. Joseph Allen, of Northborough, addressed the people. Other parts were taken by

Rev. Messrs. Calvin Lincoln, Alonzo Hill, Huntington, E. B. Wilson, R. S. Edes and W. Gilbert.

(11) The sermon at the installation of Rev. Amos Smith was preached by Rev. Ezra F. Gannett, D. D. Rev. Messrs. Calvin Lincoln, E. B. Wilson, and Dr. Parkman also participated in the services.

(12) The principal parts at the ordination of Rev. Stephen Barker were filled as follows: Rev. H. W. Bellows, D. D., preached the sermon; Rev. F. Hinckley gave the charge; Rev. E. M. Wheelock, of Dover, N. H., extended the Right Hand of Fellowship; Rev. W. P. Tilden addressed the people. Rev. Messrs. T. T. Stone, James Thurston, W. H. Knapp and E. M. Bartol also participated.

(13) At the installation of Rev. Eli Fay, Rev. Rufus P. Stebbins, D. D., then of Woburn, preached the sermon. The installing prayer was made by Rev. Alonzo Hill, D. D. Rev. Horatio Stebbins, of Portland, gave the charge, and Rev. W. P. Tilden tendered the Fellowship of the churches. Rev. R. R. Shippen addressed the society.

(14) Rev. J. B. Green's installation was conducted by the following clergymen: Rev. Geo. Putnam, of Roxbury, preached the sermon; Rev. Stillman Barber extended the Right Hand of Fellowship, and the charge was given by Rev. Joseph Allen, D. D. Rev. Alonzo Hill, D. D., made the installing prayer, while the address to the people was made by Rev. Geo. S. Ball. Rev. Messrs. Shippen, Bartol and Brown, also assisted.

(15) The ordination of E. A. Horton was participated in by the following clergymen: Rev. James Freeman Clarke, D. D., preached the sermon. Rev. W. S. Heywood gave the charge; Rev. C. Nightingale, addressed the people; Rev. G. H. Young extended the Right Hand of Fellowship and Rev. Joseph Allen, D. D., made the ordaining prayer. Rev Messrs Nickerson and Browne took parts.

(16) The committee on building the Chapel were J. H. Lockey, and Howard M. Lane.

(17) These changes were quite significant. The choir seats were transferred to a recess behind the pulpit; one hundred new seats were thus secured, making in all nearly 900 sittings. Gas was introduced, new frescoing entirely made, the old carpet displaced by a new one, a modern platform and desk substituted for the former pulpit, and the steep entrance steps altered to an easy and gradual ascent. These and other alterations were made at a cost of about $6000.

(18) For reference, I have placed the list of pastorates of this society,— the majority of which were since the erection of this structure, in one table. Eleven pastors has this society had, including the present one.

John Rogers was pastor 15 years, from 1743 to 1758.

Francis Gardner, 52 years; from 1762 to 1814.

Wm. Bascom, 5 years; from 1815 to 1820.
Abel Conant, 15 years; from 1820 to 1836.
Rufus P. Stebbins, 7 years; from 1837 to 1843.
Hiram Withington, 4 years; from 1844 to 1848.
Amos Smith, 8 years; from 1848 to 1856.
Stephen Barker, 3 years; from 1857 to 1860.
Eli Fay, 3 years; from 1861 to 1864.
J. B. Green, 3 years; 1864 to 1867.

(A) Possibly it may not be uninteresting to state the dates of the dedication of all other Meeting-houses in this town.

The Evangelical Society dedicated its first house of worship in 1824. It was that building now occupied by the Catholics. Their second one was dedicated February 8th, 1837, and their third, being the present one, standing where the second one did, was consecrated this year, August 15.

The Baptist society dedicated its first house in June, 1832. It was located on the North Village road between the two villages, and was at one time occupied by the Catholics. On June 2d, 1850, this people dedicated a new one which is their present house of worship, built on land purchased of this parish.

The first Meeting-house occupied by the Methodists was placed at the junction of the Shirley and Harvard roads, in the North Village, dedicated 1829. They afterwards bought the Evangelical Society's house of worship, on Main Street, and used it for the first time in January, 1839. Their present edifice was dedicated in 1873.

The Catholics having occupied the former Baptist house at infrequent times, finally sold it and purchased the Methodist Meeting-House in 1871, which they now occupy. That building has thus been tenanted by three different denominations.

(B) Appended is a list of the Superintendents of our S. School, since its organization in 1838:

Solon Carter served from 1838 to 1850; Luke Lincoln from 1850 to 1855; Abel C. Wilder, from 1855 to 1865; Porter M. Kimball, 1865 to 1866; Chauncy W. Carter, 1866 to 1868; Frank C. Bowen was elected April 16th, 1868, and now serves.

(C) For many valuable facts and statistics relating to the church, the early inhabitants, and past ecclesiastical transactions in Leominster, the reader may profitably consult David Wilder's History of the Town, Dr. Stebbins' Centennial Discourse on the organization of the First Congregational Church, and some pamphlets and papers deposited in the Museum archives; an institution as yet young and scant in materials, but destined, I hope, to be the repository of much local historical matter. There is a great need, already, of a well written history of Leominster. By a little care now, in saving the material, some future writer will be able to prepare his work from satisfactory data.

www.ingramcontent.com/pod-product-compliance
Lightning Source LLC
Chambersburg PA
CBHW021457090426
42739CB00009B/1764